ARMISTICE

ARMISTICE

A Laureate's Choice of Poems of War and Peace

edited by

CAROL ANN DUFFY

FABER & FABER

First published in 2018
by Faber & Faber Ltd
Bloomsbury House
74–77 Great Russell Street
London WC1B 3DA

Typeset by Typo•glyphix
Printed in the UK by TJ International Ltd, Padstow, Cornwall

A CIP record for this book
is available from the British Library

ISBN 978–0–571–34707–0

MIX
Paper from
responsible sources
FSC® C013056

CONTENTS

Foreword

The word 'armistice' derives from the Latin *'arma'* (meaning weapons) and *'stitium'* (meaning a stoppage or suspension). It stands for a moment of pause in the fight, opening up space for dialogue and the coming together of warring sides. Unlike a ceasefire, which can be any temporary halt in hostilities, a call for armistice carries with it a formally shared hope of striving towards and settling upon a more secure and lasting state of peace. As we mark the hundred years since the signing of the Armistice on 11 November 1918, which ended the fighting between the Allies and Germany, this anthology of poems remembers not only the Great War and its soldiers and poets, but uses the idea of armistice as a light to look at other moments of conflict and peace both before and after 1914–1918.

From Ancient Greece to the Troubles of Northern Ireland, the poets of these pages write, across centuries, of the grief of war and the bruised grace of peace. The laying down of arms at one time and place is all too soon followed by conflict elsewhere. As Wisława Szymborska acknowledges here, 'All the cameras have gone / to other wars'. The soldiers who returned home injured after 'the war to end all wars' are mirrored in John Balaban's post-Vietnam poem, where 'all across the USA / the wounded walk about and wonder where to go'. In the one hundred poems here, some of them specially commissioned for this anthology, what is striking is the poets' urgent valuing of the commonplace in the aftermath of war: Sara Teasdale's robins 'whistling their whims on a low fence-wire'; Charlotte Mew's wounded trees, waiting 'with their old wise patience for the heavenly rain'; and Freda Laughton's 'bland smile of eggs in the willow-basket'. Among the anguish, bitterness and anger, Ivan Lalić's 'spaces of hope' make room for armistice. We can see in these pages that, if war is the messenger of hate, poetry is the messenger of love.

I would like to thank Matthew Hollis and Lavinia Singer at Faber for their help in preparing this anthology, and Ella Duffy for collaborating with me in researching many of the poems.

CAROL ANN DUFFY

ARMISTICE

SARA TEASDALE

There Will Come Soft Rains

There will come soft rains and the smell of the ground,
And swallows calling with their shimmering sound;

And frogs in the pools singing at night,
And wild-plum trees in tremulous white;

Robins will wear their feathery fire
Whistling their whims on a low fence-wire;

And not one will know of the war, not one
Will care at last when it is done.

Not one would mind, neither bird nor tree,
If mankind perished utterly;

And Spring herself, when she woke at dawn,
Would scarcely know that we were gone.

Everyone Sang

Everyone suddenly burst out singing;
And I was filled with such delight
As prisoned birds must find in freedom,
Winging wildly across the white
Orchards and dark-green fields; on – on – and out of sight.

Everyone's voice was suddenly lifted;
And beauty came like the setting sun:
My heart was shaken with tears; and horror
Drifted away . . . O, but Everyone
Was a bird; and the song was wordless; the singing will
    never be done.

RUTH PITTER

The Military Harpist

Strangely assorted, the shape of song and the bloody man.

Under the harp's gilt shoulder and rainlike strings,
Prawn-eyed, with prawnlike bristle, well-waxed moustache,
With long tight cavalry legs, and the spurred boot
Ready upon the swell, the Old Sweat waits.

Now dies, and dies hard, the stupid, well-relished fortissimo,
Wood-wind alone inviting the liquid tone,
The voice of the holy and uncontending, the harp.

Ceasing to ruminate interracial fornications,
He raises his hands, and his wicked old mug is David's,
Pastoral, rapt, the king and the poet in innocence,
Singing Saul in himself asleep, and the ancient Devil
Clean out of countenance, as with an army of angels.

He is now where his bunion has no existence.
Breathing an atmosphere free of pipeclay and swearing,
He wears the starched nightshirt of the hereafter, his halo
Is plain manly brass with a permanent polish,
Requiring no oily rag and no Soldier's Friend.

His place is with the beloved poet of Israel,
With the wandering minnesinger and the loves of Provence,
With Blondel footsore and heartsore, the voice in
     the darkness
Crying like beauty bereaved beneath many a donjon,
O Richard! O king! where is the lion of England?
With Howell, Llewellyn, and far in the feral north
With the savage fame of the hero in glen and in ben,
At the morning discourse of saints in the island Eire,
And at nameless doings in the stone-circle, the
     dreadful grove.

Thus far into the dark do I delve for his likeness:
He harps at the Druid sacrifice, where the golden string
Sings to the golden knife and the victim's shriek.
Strangely assorted, the shape of song and the bloody man.

MARION ANGUS

Remembrance Day

Some one was singing
    Up a twisty stair,
    A fragment of a song,
    One sweet, spring day,
When twelve o'clock was ringing,
    Through the sunny square –

'There was a lad baith frank and free,
Cam' doon the bonnie banks o' Dee
Wi' tartan plaid and buckled shoon,
An' he'll come nae mair to oor toon.' –

'He dwells within a far countree,
Where great ones do him courtesie,
They've gien him a golden croon,
An' he'll come nae mair to oor toon.' –

No one is singing
    Up the twisty stair.
Quiet as a sacrament
    The November day.

Can't you hear it swinging,
    The little ghostly air? –
    Hear it sadly stray
    Through the misty square,
In and out a doorway,
    Up a twisty stair –
Tartan plaid and buckled shoon,
He'll come nae mair to oor toon.

MAHMOUD DARWISH

Murdered and Unknown

Murdered, and unknown. No forgetfulness gathers them
and no remembrance scatters them . . . they're forgotten in
winter's grass on the public highway between
two long stories about heroism and suffering.
'I am the victim.' 'No. I alone am
the victim.' They didn't tell the author: 'No
victim kills another. There is in
the story a victim and a killer.' They were young
picking the snow off Christ's cypress,
and playing with cherubs, since they were
of one generation . . . they used to leak out
of schools to escape math and ancient
Hamassa poetry, then play with soldiers,
by the roadblocks, the innocent game of death.
They didn't tell the soldiers: 'Drop your rifles
and open up the roads for the butterfly to find
its mother by morning, and for us to fly with
the butterfly outside dreams, since dreams
are narrow at our doors.' They were young
playing, and making a story for the red
rose beneath the snow, behind two long
stories about heroism and suffering, and they were
running away with cherubs toward a clear sky.

translated by FADY JOUDAH

9

WISŁAWA SZYMBORSKA

The End and the Beginning

After every war
someone has to tidy up.
Things won't pick
themselves up, after all.

Someone has to shove
the rubble to the roadsides
so the carts loaded with corpses
can get by.

Someone has to trudge
through sludge and ashes,
through the sofa springs,
the shards of glass,
the bloody rags.

Someone has to lug the post
to prop the wall,
someone has to glaze the window,
set the door in its frame.

No sound bites, no photo opportunities,
and it takes years.
All the cameras have gone
to other wars.

The bridges need to be rebuilt,
the railroad stations, too.
Shirtsleeves will be rolled
to shreds.

Someone, broom in hand,
still remembers how it was.
Someone else listens, nodding
his unshattered head.
But others are bound to be bustling nearby
who'll find all that
a little boring.

From time to time someone still must
dig up a rusted argument
from underneath a bush
and haul it off to the dump.

Those who knew
what this was all about
must make way for those
who know little.
And less than that.
And at last nothing less than nothing.

Someone has to lie there
in the grass that covers up
the causes and effects
with a cornstalk in his teeth,
gawking at clouds.

translated by STANISŁAW BARAŃCZAK *and*
CLARE CAVANAGH

The Bugle

High over London
Victory floats
And high, high, high,
Harsh bugle notes
Rend and embronze the air.
Triumph is there
With sombre sunbeams mixed of Autumn rare.
Over and over the loud brass makes its cry,
Summons to exultancy
Of past in Victory.
Yet in the gray street women void of grace
Chatter of trifles
Hurry to barter, wander aimlessly
The heedless town,
Men lose their souls in care of business,
As men had not been mown
Like corn swathes East of Ypres or the Somme
Never again home
Or beauty most beloved to see, for that
London Town might still be busy at
Its sordid cares
Traffic of wares.
O Town, O Town
In soldiers' faces one might see the fear

That once again they should be called to bear
Arms, and to save England from her own.

For a Girl

Paris, November 11 1918

Go cheering down the boulevards
And shout and wave your flags,
Go dancing down the boulevards
In all your gladdest rags:
And raise your cheers and wave your flags
And kiss the passer-by,
But let me break my heart in peace
For all the best men die.
    It was 'When the War is over
    Our dreams will all come true,
    When the War is over
    I'll come back to you';
    And the War is over, over,
    And they never can come true.

Go cheering down the boulevards
In all your brave array,
Go singing down the boulevards
To celebrate the day:
But for God's sake let me stay at home
And break my heart and cry,
I've loved and worked, and I'll be glad,
But all the best men die.

It was 'When the War is over
Our dreams will all come true,
When the War is over
I'll come back to you';
And the War is over, over,
And they never can come true.

IOAN ALEXANDRU

The End of the War

When I came into the world the war was endin',
Last orders were shot. On field
Last cannons were hung by their shadows.
In our house presents were shared.

'First to you, John,' said the War to father, from the corner
    of the table,
'Because you have served me so faithfully
I hand you this wooden leg.
Wear it in memory of me, and good health to you.
It's sturdy from the trunk of an old oak;
When you die the woods will rock you
Like a brother in the summits of their eyes.
Your right hand, because it has no book learning anyway,
I wrenched from your elbow and have given it to the earth
To teach it to write.

'For you, Maria,' said the War to my mother –
'Because you watered my horses with your tears
And left two sons on the battlefield
To polish my boots, and brought up
Two maidens with whom I've spent my nights,
Look, I'll give you this beautiful bunch of wakeful nights,
As well as this empty house without a roof.

To you, George, son of Peter from over the hill, –
For those two hazel eyes, you say you had,
Look, I give you possession of all the boundaries
    of darkness,
So you can harvest them, you and your wife
Forever.

'For the village I leave only forty orphans
Under six months, ten empty houses and the others in ruins,
Also, the sky towards sunset, half-burned.
The tower without bells; eight women in the cemetery
Hung with heads to the ground, and twenty horses dead
    from the neighbour's farm.

'For you, just born, because we don't know each other
    very well,
I leave the cow's udder dry,
The plum trees burned alive in the garden,
The eye of the well, dead,
And may the sky feed you on its stars.
And I baptise you in the name of the Lord.'

translated by ANDREA DELETANT *and* BRENDA WALKER

AMY LOWELL

Convalescence

From out the dragging vastness of the sea,
　　Wave-fettered, bound in sinuous seaweed strands,
　　He toils toward the rounding beach, and stands
One moment, white and dripping, silently,
Cut like a cameo in lazuli,
　　Then falls, betrayed by shifting shells, and lands
　　Prone in the jeering water, and his hands
Clutch for support where no support can be.
　　So up, and down, and forward, inch by inch,
He gains upon the shore, where poppies glow
And sandflies dance their little lives away.
　　The sucking waves retard, and tighter clinch
The weeds about him, but the land-winds blow,
And in the sky there blooms the sun of May.

The Pomegranates of Kandahar

The bald heft of ordnance
A landmine
shrapnel cool in its shell

Red balls
pinioned in pyramids
rough deal tables stacked to the sky

A mirrored shawl
splits
and dozens tumble down –

careering through the marketplace
joyful fruit
caught by the shouts of barefoot children

Assembled, they are jewels –
jewels
of garnet, jewels of ruby

A promise deep as the deep red of poppies
of rouged lips (concealed)
Proud hearts

built of rubble
Come, let us light candles in the dust
and prise them apart –

thrust your knife through the globe
then twist
till the soft flesh cleaves open

to these small shards of sweetness
Tease each jellied cell
from its white fur of membrane

till a city explodes in your mouth
Harvest of goodness,
harvest of blood

Ambulance Train 30

A.T. 30 lies in the siding.
Above her cold grey clouds lie, silver-long as she.
Like a great battleship that never saw defeat
She dreams: while the pale day dies down
Behind the harbour town,
Beautiful, complete
And unimpassioned as the long grey sea.

A.T. 30 lies in the siding.
Gone are her red crosses – the sick that were her own.
Like a great battleship that never saw defeat
She waits, while the pale day dies down
Behind the harbour town,
Beautiful, complete . . .
And the Occupying Army boards her for Cologne.

May 6, 1919

Progress

They say that for years Belfast was backwards
and it's great now to see some progress.
So I guess we can look forward to taking boxes
from the earth. I guess that ambulances
will leave the dying back amidst the rubble
to be explosively healed. Given time,
one hundred thousand particles of glass
will create impossible patterns in the air
before coalescing into the clarity
of a window. Through which, a reassembled head
will look out and admire the shy young man
taking his bomb from the building and driving home.

from Freehold

Townland of Peace

Once in a showery summer, sick of war,
I strode the roads that slanted to Kilmore,
that church-topped mound where half the tombstones wear
my people's name; some notion drew me there,
illogical, but not to be ignored,
some need of roots saluted, some sought word
that might give strength and sense to my slack rein,
by this directed, not to lose again
the line and compass so my head and heart
no longer plunge and tug to drag apart.

Thus walking dry or sheltered under trees,
I stepped clean out of Europe into peace,
for every man I met was relevant
to the harsh clamour of my eager want,
gathering fruit, or leading horse uphill,
sawing his timber, measuring his well.
The crooked apple trees beside the gate
that almost touched the roadside with the weight
of their clenched fruit, the dappled calves that browsed
free in the netted sunlight and unhoused
the white hens slouching round the tar-bright sheds,
the neat-leafed damsons with the smoky beads,

the farm unseen but loud with bucket and dog
and voices moving in a leafy fog,
gave neither hint nor prophecy of change,
save the slow seasons in their circled range;
part of a world of natural diligence
that has forgotten its old turbulence,
save when the spade rasps on a rusted sword
or a child in a schoolbook finds a savage word.

Old John, my father's father, ran these roads
a hundred years ago with other lads
up the steep brae to school, or over the stile
to the far house for milk, or dragging the long mile
to see his mother buried. Every stride
with gable, gatepost, hedge on either side,
companioned so brought nearer my desire
to stretch my legs beside a poet's fire
in the next parish. As the road went by
with meadow and orchard, under a close sky,
and stook-lined field, and thatched and slated house
and apples heavy on the crouching boughs,
I moved beside him. Change was strange and far
where a daft world gone shabby choked with war
among the crumpled streets or in the plains
spiked with black fire-crisped rafters and buckled lines,
from Warsaw to the Yangtze, where the slow-
phrased people learn such thought that scourge and blow
may school them into strength to find the skill
for new societies of earth and steel,
but here's the age they've lost.

                                 The boys I met
munching their windfalls, drifting homeward late,
are like that boy a hundred years ago,
the same bare kibes, the heirloom rags they show;
but they must take another road in time.
Across the sea his fortune summoned him
to the brave heyday of the roaring mills
where progress beckoned with a million wheels.

[. . .]

Now and for ever through the change-rocked years,
I know my corner in the universe;
my corner, this small region limited
in space by sea, in the time by my own dead,
who are its compost, by each roving sense
henceforward mobilised in its defence,
against the sickness that has struck mankind,
mass-measured, mass-infected, mass-resigned.

Against the anthill and the beehive state
I hold the right of man to stay out late,
to sulk and laugh, to criticise or pray,
when he is moved, at any hour of day,
to vote by show of hands or sit at home,
or stroll on Sunday with a vasculum,
to sing or act or play or paint or write
in any mode that offers him delight.

I hold my claim against the mammoth powers
to crooked roads and accidental flowers,
to corn with poppies fabulously red,
to trout in rivers, and to wheat in bread,
to food unpoisoned, unpolluted air,
and easy pensioned age without a care
other than time's mortality must bring
to any shepherd, commissar, or king.

But these small rights require a smaller stage
than the vast forum of the nations' rage,
for they imply a well-compacted space
where every voice declares its native place,
townland, townquarter county at the most,
the local word not ignorantly lost
in the smooth jargon, bland and half alive,
which wears no clinging burr upon its sleeve
to tell the ground it grew from, and to prove
there is for sure a plot of earth we love.

Under the Greenwood Tree

Under the greenwood tree
Who loves to lie with me,
And turn his merry note
Unto the sweet bird's throat,
Come hither, come hither, come hither:
Here shall he see
No enemy
But winter and rough weather.

Who doth ambition shun
And loves to live i' the sun,
Seeking the food he eats,
And pleased with what he gets,
Come hither, come hither, come hither:
Here shall he see
No enemy
But winter and rough weather.

CHARLOTTE MEW

May, 1915

Let us remember Spring will come again
          To the scorched, blackened woods, where the
          wounded trees
Wait with their old wise patience for the heavenly rain,
Sure of the sky: sure of the sea to send its healing breeze,
          Sure of the sun. And even as to these
                    Surely the Spring, when God shall please,
          Will come again like a divine surprise
To those who sit to-day with their great Dead, hands in their
     hands, eyes in their eyes,
At one with Love, at one with Grief: blind to the scattered
     things and changing skies.

JOHN BALABAN

In Celebration of Spring

Our Asian war is over; others have begun.
Our elders, who tried to mortgage lies,
are disgraced, or dead, and already
the brokers are picking their pockets
for the keys and the credit cards.

In delta swamp in a united Vietnam,
a Marine with a bullfrog for a face,
rots in equatorial heat. An eel
slides through the cage of his bared ribs.
At night, on the old battlefield, ghosts,
like patches of fog, lurk into villages
to maunder on doorsills of cratered homes,
while all across the USA
the wounded walk about and wonder where to go.

And today, in the simmer of lyric sunlight,
the chrysalis pulses in its mushy cocoon,
under the bark on a gnarled root of an elm.
In the brilliant creek, a minnow flashes
delirious with gnats. The turtle's heart
quickens its raps in the warm bank sludge.
As she chases a frisbee spinning in sunlight,
a girl's breasts bounce full and strong;
a boy's stomach, as he turns, is flat and strong.

Swear by the locust, by dragonflies on ferns,
by the minnow's flash, the tremble of a breast,
by the new earth spongy under our feet;
that as we grow old, we will not grow evil,
that although our garden seeps with sewage,
and our elders think it's up for auction – swear
by this dazzle that does not wish to leave us –
that we will be keepers of a garden, nonetheless.

Peace

When will you ever, Peace, wild wood dove, shy wings shut,
Your round me roaming end, and under be my boughs?
When, when, Peace, will you, Peace? I'll not play hypocrite
To own my heart: I yield you do come sometimes; but
That piecemeal peace is poor peace. What pure peace allows
Alarms of wars, the daunting wars, the death of it?

O surely, reaving Peace, my Lord should leave in lieu
Some good! And so he does leave patience exquisite,
That plumes to peace thereafter. And when Peace here
   does house
He comes with work to do, he does not come to coo,
   He comes to brood and sit.

At the British War Cemetery, Bayeux

I walked where in their talking graves
And shirts of earth five thousand lay,
When history with ten feasts of fire
Had eaten the red air away.

I am Christ's boy, I cried, I bear
In iron hands the bread, the fishes.
I hang with honey and with rose
This tidy wreck of all your wishes.

On your geometry of sleep
The chestnut and the fir-tree fly,
And lavender and marguerite
Forge with their flowers an English sky.

Turn now towards the belling town
Your jigsaws of impossible bone,
And rising read your rank of snow
Accurate as death upon the stone.

About your easy heads my prayers
I said with syllables of clay.
What gift, I asked, shall I bring now
Before I weep and walk away?

Take, they replied, the oak and laurel.
Take our fortune of tears and live
Like a spendthrift lover. All we ask
Is the one gift you cannot give.

SEAN O'BRIEN

The Sunken Road

Private Harry Reed, d. 24 December 1915

I mean to walk down the sunken lane
Where the dead are once more
Trying to assemble in the dark.

By the light of Bavarian gentians
I'll be looking for the dugout
At the entrance to the mine

And then descend the deepest shaft
Where the ancient ordnance
Sweats and waits implacably

For Zero Hour beneath the ridge.
I will surface in the middle of the wood
While the teams of machine-gunners

Sleep with their heads on the barrels
Just for a minute, a minute
Before the beginning, the end,

The balloon going up, the whistles
Like a cloud of nightingales.
I carry a letter from home,

The cigarette case that will save me,
A picture of you, all the time in the world
To stroke your face, while you are waiting,

Robinette or English Rose, so patiently
There at the edge of the village
Where wildflowers grow by the road.

WILFRED OWEN

Greater Love

Red lips are not so red
    As the stained stones kissed by the English dead.
Kindness of wooed and wooer
Seems shame to their love pure.
O Love, your eyes lose lure
    When I behold eyes blinded in my stead!

Your slender attitude
    Trembles not exquisite like limbs knife-skewed,
Rolling and rolling there
Where God seems not to care;
Till the fierce love they bear
    Cramps them in death's extreme decrepitude.

Your voice sings not so soft, –
    Though even as wind murmuring through raftered loft, –
Your dear voice is not dear,
Gentle, and evening clear,
As theirs whom none now hear,
    Now earth has stopped their piteous mouths that coughed.

Heart, you were never hot
    Nor large, nor full like hearts made great with shot;
And though your hand be pale,
Paler are all which trail
Your cross through flame and hail:
    Weep, you may weep, for you may touch them not.

Dirge Without Music

I am not resigned to the shutting away of loving hearts in
    the hard ground.
So it is, and so it will be, for so it has been, time out of mind:
Into the darkness they go, the wise and the lovely. Crowned
With lilies and with laurel they go; but I am not resigned.

Lovers and thinkers, into the earth with you.
Be one with the dull, the indiscriminate dust.
A fragment of what you felt, of what you knew,
A formula, a phrase remains, – but the best is lost.

The answers quick and keen, the honest look, the laughter,
    the love, –
They are gone. They are gone to feed the roses. Elegant
    and curled
Is the blossom. Fragrant is the blossom. I know. But I do
    not approve.
More precious was the light in your eyes than all the roses
    in the world.

Down, down, down into the darkness of the grave
Gently they go, the beautiful, the tender, the kind;
Quietly they go, the intelligent, the witty, the brave.
I know. But I do not approve. And I am not resigned.

Reconciliation

When you are standing at your hero's grave,
Or near some homeless village where he died,
Remember, through your heart's rekindling pride,
The German soldiers who were loyal and brave.

Men fought like brutes; and hideous things were done;
And you have nourished hatred, harsh and blind.
But in that Golgotha perhaps you'll find
The Mothers of the men that killed your son.

November, 1918

Reconciliation

Word over all, beautiful as the sky,
Beautiful that war and all its deeds of carnage must in
    time be utterly lost,
That the hands of the sisters Death and Night
    incessantly softly wash again, and ever again, this
    soiled world;
For my enemy is dead, a man divine as myself is dead,
I look where he lies white-faced and still in the coffin –
    I draw near,
Bend down and touch lightly with my lips the white
    face in the coffin.

Two Fusiliers

And have we done with War at last?
Well, we've been lucky devils both,
And there's no need of pledge or oath
To bind our lovely friendship fast,
By firmer stuff
Close bound enough.

By wire and wood and stake we're bound,
By Fricourt and by Festubert,
By whipping rain, by the sun's glare,
By all the misery and loud sound,
By a Spring day,
By Picard clay.

Show me the two so closely bound
As we, by the wet bond of blood,
By friendship blossoming from mud,
By Death: we faced him, and we found
Beauty in Death,
In dead men, breath.

Truce

It begins with one or two soldiers
And one or two following
With hampers over their shoulders.
They might be off wildfowling

As they would another Christmas Day,
So gingerly they pick their steps.
No one seems sure of what to do.
All stop when one stops.

A fire gets lit. Some spread
Their greatcoats on the frozen ground.
Polish vodka, fruit and bread
Are broken out and passed round.

The air of an old German song,
The rules of Patience, are the secrets
They'll share before long.
They draw on their last cigarettes

As Friday-night lovers, when it's over,
Might get up from their mattresses
To congratulate each other
And exchange names and addresses.

The Handshake

Spied through a soggy sheep's-wool November mist
the two duellists looked to be standing too close.
'Touching distance' a poet wrote in his book,
his head periscoping over the flooded trench.

Bets were placed on who'd be the first to blink.
Then one man released an unholstered mitt
from his wrist, which flapped into the breach
and hovered there, prompting the other's unfurled fist

to swim slowly forward out of his dark sleeve.
Another poet, standing on piled sandbags
of dead friends, swore he'd seen them meet and mate –
the rude pink bird and the raw pink fish.

Hard to say, though, scanning through shattered glass
across commons drifting with flags and saints.

SAPPHO

To an Army Wife in Sardis

Some say a cavalry troop,
others say an infantry, and others, still,
will swear that the swift oars

of our sea fleet are the best
sight on dark earth; but I say
that whomever one loves is.

translation adapted by DANIELA GIOSEFFI

45

EDNA ST VINCENT MILLAY

Conscientious Objector

I shall die, but that is all that I shall do for Death.

I hear him leading his horse out of the stall; I hear the
    clatter on the barn-floor.
He is in haste; he has business in Cuba, business in the
    Balkans, many calls to make this morning.
But I will not hold the bridle while he cinches the girth.
And he may mount by himself; I will not give him a leg up.

Though he flick my shoulders with his whip, I will not tell
    him which way the fox ran.
With his hoof on my breast, I will not tell him where the
    black boy hides in the swamp.
I shall die, but that is all that I shall do for Death; I am not
    on his pay-roll.

I will not tell him the whereabouts of my friends nor of my
    enemies either,
Though he promise me much, I will not map him the route
    to any man's door.
Am I a spy in the land of the living, that I should deliver
    men to Death?
Brother, the password and plans of our city are safe with
    me; never through me
Shall you be overcome.

SAADI YOUSSEF

Night in Al-Hamra

A candle on the long road
A candle in the slumbering houses
A candle for the terrified stores
A candle for the bakeries
A candle for the journalist shuddering in an empty office
A candle for the fighter
A candle for the doctor at the sick bed
A candle for the wounded
A candle for honest talk
A candle for staircases
A candle for the hotel crowded with refugees
A candle for the singer
A candle for the broadcasters in a shelter
A candle for a bottle of water
A candle for the air
A candle for two lovers in a stripped apartment
A candle for the sky that has folded
A candle for the beginning
A candle for the end
A candle for the final decision
A candle for conscience
A candle in my hand

translated by KHALED MATTAWA

47

The Cenotaph

September 1919

Not yet will those measureless fields be green again
Where only yesterday the wild sweet blood of wonderful
 youth was shed;
There is a grave whose earth must hold too long, too deep
 a stain,
Though for ever over it we may speak as proudly as we
 may tread.
But here, where the watchers by lonely hearths from the
 thrust of an inward sword have more slowly bled,
We shall build the Cenotaph: Victory, winged, with Peace,
 winged too, at the column's head.
And over the stairway, at the foot – oh! here, leave desolate,
 passionate hands to spread
Violets, roses, and laurel, with the small, sweet, twinkling
 country things
Speaking so wistfully of other Springs,
From the little gardens of little places where son or
 sweetheart was born and bred.
In splendid sleep, with a thousand brothers
 To lovers – to mothers
 Here, too, lies he:
Under the purple, the green, the red,

It is all young life: it must break some women's hearts to see
Such a brave, gay coverlet to such a bed!
Only, when all is done and said,
God is not mocked and neither are the dead.
For this will stand in our Market-place –
                    Who'll sell, who'll buy
                    (Will you or I
Lie each to each with the better grace)?
While looking into every busy whore's and huckster's face
As they drive their bargains, is the Face
Of God: and some young, piteous, murdered face.

Penelope

In the pathway of the sun,
   In the footsteps of the breeze,
Where the world and sky are one,
   He shall ride the silver seas,
      He shall cut the glittering wave.
I shall sit at home, and rock;
Rise, to heed a neighbour's knock;
Brew my tea, and snip my thread;
Bleach the linen for my bed.
     They will call him brave.

Abou Ben Adhem and the Angel

Abou Ben Adhem (may his tribe increase!)
Awoke one night from a deep dream of peace,
And saw, within the moonlight in his room,
Making it rich, and like a lily in bloom,
An angel writing in a book of gold: –
Exceeding peace had made Ben Adhem bold,
And to the presence in the room he said,
    'What writest thou?' – The vision raised its head,
And with a look made of all sweet accord,
Answered, 'The names of those who love the Lord.'
'And is mine one?' said Abou. 'Nay, not so,'
Replied the angel. Abou spoke more low,
But cheerly still; and said, 'I pray thee, then,
Write me as one that loves his fellow men.'

    The angel wrote, and vanished. The next night
It came again with a great wakening light,
And showed the names whom love of God had blest,
And lo! Ben Adhem's name led all the rest!

Making Peace

A voice from the dark called out,
         'The poets must give us
imagination of peace, to oust the intense, familiar
imagination of disaster. Peace, not only
the absence of war.'
                  But peace, like a poem,
it is not there ahead of itself,
can't be imagined before it is made,
can't be known except
in the words of its making,
grammar of justice,
syntax of mutual aid.
                  A feeling towards it,
dimly sensing a rhythm, is all we have
until we begin to utter its metaphors,
learning them as we speak.
                        A line of peace might appear
if we restructured the sentence our lives are making,
revoked its reaffirmation of profit and power,
questioned our needs, allowed
long pauses . . .
                  A cadence of peace might balance its weight
on that different fulcrum; peace a presence,
an energy field more intense than war,
might pulse then,

stanza by stanza into the world,
each of living
one of its words, each word
a vibration of light – facets
of the forming crystal.

Stronghold

In your fortress arms
I will never die
I will fear no evil
Terror will not strike me
I will not hear
The creaking in the night
The loaded wheels
Moving through the battlefield.

A safe stronghold
Your arms around me
Your broad shoulders
Shielding me from fate
Finding me a shelter
From the keen wind of life –
There is a secret garden
Between your shoulderblades.

And in that garden
There are bees and olive-trees
There is honey on the rushes
And the trees all in flower.
In the early Autumn
– Winter never comes there

And the frosty breezes
Never blow there at all.

And beyond our circle
There are countries, peoples
Fighting, founding dynasties
Multiplying on the globe
If the four corners
Of the earth were one flame
If the whole universe
Were to fizz and explode

I couldn't care, your arms
Still solid around me,
No place for terror
No room for hunger.
When you fold me
In your gentle embrace
I am as safe and sound
As that city on a mountain

Hold me in your strong
Conjuring circle
With the heat of your body
The warmed, sound frame,
Your skin on my skin
Mouth on my mouth firmly
I will not hear the wolves
Howling on the plain.

All things are temporary
In half an hour
You'll kiss my forehead
And turn away and sleep
Leaving me on my side
Of the double bed
Reminded of sudden death
And building a wall against fear.

from the Irish of NUALA NÍ DHOMHNAILL

The Peace of Wild Things

When despair for the world grows in me
and I wake in the night at the least sound
in fear of what my life and my children's lives may be,
I go and lie down where the wood drake
rests in his beauty on the water, and the great heron feeds.
I come into the peace of wild things
who do not tax their lives with forethought
of grief. I come into the presence of still water.
And I feel above me the day-blind stars
waiting with their light. For a time
I rest in the grace of the world, and am free.

Grass

Pile the bodies high at Austerlitz and Waterloo.
Shovel them under and let me work —
　　　　I am the grass; I cover all.

And pile them high at Gettysburg
And pile them high at Ypres and Verdun.
Shovel them under and let me work,
Two years, ten years, and passengers ask the conductor:
　　　　What place in this?
　　　　Where are we now?

　　　　I am the grass.
　　　　Let me work.

HELEN WADDELL

April 20th, 1939
(Hitler is to address the Reichstag on April 28th)

Earth said to Death,
Give these a little breath.
Give them eight days to feel the sun,
To see the limes in leaf . . .
Give me eight days,
And I will pour the silence of June
Into this April noon,
Wine of October in the vine still curled.
Then let you come.
Darkness shall find them sleeping undismayed,
Who shall make them afraid
Who saw eternity
In the brief compass of an April day?

SHERMAN ALEXIE

The Powwow at the End of the World

I am told by many of you that I must forgive and so I shall
after an Indian woman puts her shoulder to the Grand Coulee Dam
and topples it. I am told by many of you that I must forgive
and so I shall after the floodwaters burst each successive dam
downriver from the Grand Coulee. I am told by many of you
that I must forgive and so I shall after the floodwaters find
their way to the mouth of the Columbia River as it enters the Pacific
and causes all of it to rise. I am told by many of you that I
    must forgive
and so I shall after the first drop of floodwater is swallowed by
    that salmon
waiting in the Pacific. I am told by many of you that I must forgive
    and so I shall
after that salmon swims upstream, through the mouth of
    the Columbia
and then past the flooded cities, broken dams and
    abandoned reactors
of Hanford. I am told by many of you that I must forgive and so
    I shall
after that salmon swims through the mouth of the Spokane River
as it meets the Columbia, then upstream, until it arrives
in the shallows of a secret bay on the reservation where I wait alone.
I am told by many of you that I must forgive and so I shall after
that salmon leaps into the night air above the water, throws
a lightning bolt at the brush near my feet, and starts the fire

which will lead all of the lost Indians home. I am told
by many of you that I must forgive and so I shall
after we Indians have gathered around the fire with that salmon
who has three stories it must tell before sunrise: one story will
    teach us
how to pray; another story will make us laugh for hours;
the third story will give us reason to dance. I am told by many
of you that I must forgive and so I shall when I am dancing
with my tribe during the powwow at the end of the world.

Ceasefire

I

Put in mind of his own father and moved to tears
Achilles took him by the hand and pushed the old king
Gently away, but Priam curled up at his feet and
Wept with him until their sadness filled the building.

II

Taking Hector's corpse into his own hands Achilles
Made sure it was washed and, for the old king's sake,
Laid out in uniform, ready for Priam to carry
Wrapped like a present home to Troy at daybreak.

III

When they had eaten together, it pleased them both
To stare at each other's beauty as lovers might,
Achilles built like a god, Priam good-looking still
And full of conversation, who earlier had sighed:

IV

'I get down on my knees and do what must be done
And kiss Achilles' hand, the killer of my son.'

Reconciliation

When all the stress and all the toil is over,
And my lover lies sleeping by your lover,
With alien earth on hands and brows and feet,
    Then we may meet.

Moving sorrowfully with uneven paces,
The bright sun shining on our ravaged faces,
There, very quietly, without sound or speech,
    Each shall greet each.

We who are bound by the same grief for ever,
When all our sons are dead may talk together,
Each asking pardon from the other one
    For her dead son.

With such low, tender words the heart may fashion,
Broken and few, of pity and compassion,
Knowing that we disturb at every tread
    Our mutual dead.

The Armistice

In an Office, in Paris

The news came through over the telephone:
All the terms had been signed: the War was won:
And all the fighting and the agony,
And all the labour of the years were done.
One girl clicked sudden at her typewriter
And whispered, 'Jerry's safe', and sat and stared:
One said, 'It's over, over, it's the end:
The War is over: ended': and a third,
'I can't remember life without the war'.
And one came in and said, 'Look here, they say
We can all go at five to celebrate,
As long as two stay on, just for to-day'.

It was quite quiet in the big empty room
Among the typewriters and little piles
Of index cards: one said, 'We'd better just
Finish the day's reports and do the files'.
And said, 'It's awf'lly like *Recessional*,
Now when the tumult has all died away'.
The other said, 'Thank God we saw it through;
I wonder what they'll do at home to-day'.
And said, 'You know it will be quiet to-night
Up at the Front: first time in all these years,
And no one will be killed there any more',

And stopped, to hide her tears.
She said, 'I've told you; he was killed in June'.
The other said, 'My dear, I know; I know . . .
It's over for me too . . . My Man was killed,
Wounded . . . and died . . . at Ypres . . . three years ago . . .
And he's my Man, and I want him,' she said,
And knew that peace could not give back her Dead.

War and Peace

In sodden trenches I have heard men speak,
though numb and wretched, wise and witty things;
and loved them for the stubbornness that clings
longest to laughter when Death's pulleys creak;

and seeing cool nurses move on tireless feet
to do abominable things with grace,
dreamed them dear sisters in that haunted place
where, with child's voices, strong men howl or bleat.

Yet now those men lay stubborn courage by,
riding dull-eyed and silent in the train
to old-man stools; or sell gay-coloured socks
and listen fearfully for Death; so I
love the low-laughing girls, who now again
go daintily, in thin and flowery frocks.

Peace

My soul, there is a country
   Far beyond the stars,
Where stands a wingèd sentry
   All skilful in the wars:
There, above noise and danger,
   Sweet Peace sits crowned with smiles,
And one born in a manger
   Commands the beauteous files.
He is thy gracious friend,
   And – O my soul, awake! –
Did in pure love descend
   To die here for thy sake.
If thou canst get but thither,
   There grows the flower of Peace,
The rose that cannot wither,
   Thy fortress, and thy ease.
Leave then thy foolish ranges;
   For none can thee secure
But one who never changes –
   Thy God, thy life, thy cure.

THOMAS HARDY

Christmas: 1924

'Peace upon earth!' was said. We sing it,
And pay a million priests to bring it.
After two thousand years of mass
We've got as far as poison-gas.

LINDA PASTAN

At Gettysburg

These fields can never be
simply themselves. Their green
seems such a tender green,
their contours so significant
to the tourists who stare

towards the far range of mountains
as if they are listening
to the page of history tearing
or to what they know themselves of warfare
between brothers. In this scenery

cows and cannons stand side by side
and motionless, as if they had grown here.
The cannons on their simple wheels
resemble farm carts, children
climb them. Thus function disappears almost entirely

into form, and what is left under
the impartial blue of the sky is a landscape
where dandelions lie in the tall grass
like so many spent cartridges, turning
at last to the smoke

of puffballs; where the only red
visible comes at sunset;
where the earth has grown so lovely
it seems to forgive us even as we are learning
to forgive ourselves.

C. K. STEAD

Another Horatian Ode

Peace, great Augustus, can be yours —
    it is only an edict away:
        say 'I will not be Caesar,

'will not honour the poet who sings
    "Sweet and proper it is
        to die for one's country,"

'nor the casuist asking why
    our brothers call us, unheard
        to save them from the tyrant.'

Honour the Moon at midnight
    when she rules in shadow
        unbroken by flame or sword,

the city untouched by fire,
    the streets not running with blood,
        the forum where music sounds.

Celebrate the grape that ripens on the vine,
    the fish in the net, the lovers
        yawning at daybreak,

and the dreaming poet
    who calls upon you, Augustus,
        to be greater than you were.

MICHAEL LONGLEY

All of These People

Who was it who suggested that the opposite of war
Is not so much peace as civilisation? He knew
Our assassinated Catholic greengrocer who died
At Christmas in the arms of our Methodist minister,
And our ice-cream man whose continuing requiem
Is the twenty-one flavours children have by heart.
Our cobbler mends shoes for everybody; our butcher
Blends into his best sausages leeks, garlic, honey;
Our cornershop sells everything from bread to kindling.
Who can bring peace to people who are not civilised?
All of these people, alive or dead, are civilised.

Death is Before Me Today

Death is before me today
like health to the sick
like leaving the bedroom after sickness.

Death is before me today
like the odor of myrrh
like sitting under a cloth on a day of wind.

Death is before me today
like the odor of lotus
like sitting down on the shore of drunkenness.

Death is before me today
like the end of the rain
like man's home-coming after the wars abroad.

Death is before me today
like the sky when it clears
like a man's wish to see home after numberless years
    of captivity.

translated by W. S. MERWIN

ROSE MACAULAY

Peace
June 28th 1919

From the tennis lawn you can hear the guns going,
    Twenty miles away,
Telling the people of the home counties
    That the peace was signed to-day.
To-night there'll be feasting in the city;
    They will drink deep and eat –
Keep peace the way you planned you would keep it
    (If we got the Boche beat).
Oh, your plan and your word, they are broken,
    For you neither dine nor dance;
And there's no peace so quiet, so lasting,
    As the peace you keep in France.

You'll be needing no Covenant of Nations
    To hold your peace intact.
It does not hang on the close guarding
    Of a frail and wordy pact.
When ours screams, shattered and driven,
    Dust down the storming years,
Yours will stand stark, like a grey fortress,
    Blind to the storm's tears.

Our peace . . . your peace . . . I see neither.
    They are a dream, and a dream.
I only see you laughing on the tennis lawn;
    And brown and alive you seem,
As you stoop over the tall red foxglove,
    (It flowers again this year)
And imprison within a freckled bell
    A bee, wild with fear . . .

*

Oh, you cannot hear the noisy guns going:
    You sleep too far away.
It is nothing to you, who have your own peace,
    That our peace was signed to-day.

Song of the Rain

Night,
And the yellow pleasure of candle-light . . .
Old brown books and the kind fine face of the clock
Fogged in the veils of the fire – its cuddling tock.

The cat,
Greening her eyes on the flame-litten mat;
Wickedly wakeful she yawns at the rain
Bending the roses over the pane,
And a bird in my heart begins to sing
Over and over the same sweet thing –

Safe in the house with my boyhood's love,
And our children asleep in the attic above.

Return

This was the way that, when the war was over,
we were to pass together. You, its lover,
would make my love your land, you said, no less,
its shining levels and their loneliness,
the reedy windings of the silent stream,
your boyhood's playmate, and your childhood's dream.

The war is over now: and we can pass
this way together. Every blade of grass
is you: you are the ripples on the river:
you are the breeze in which they leap and quiver.
I find you in the evening shadows falling
athwart the fen, you in the wildfowl calling:
and all the immanent vision cannot save
my thoughts from wandering to your unknown grave.

St Ives, 1919

The War Memorial

'The very thing we want,' (said Brown),
'To make memorial for the dead,
Is something Useful for the Town.
Some cosy reading-room?' (Brown said).
Jones seconded, obese and wise;
Slow-wagging forefinger, slow-blinking eyes.
He coughed, empurpled; hoiked at phlegm.
Ladies in furs and pink old boys
All made an acquiescent noise . . .
Tears filled my eyes, all scalding. I'd seen *them*,
Fair, doomed, unheeding . . . David . . . yellow broom . . .
And suddenly I shouldered out of the room,
Left them all gaping.

Afterwards

Oh, my beloved, shall you and I
Ever be young again, be young again?
The people that were resigned said to me
– Peace will come and you will lie
Under the larches up in Sheer,
Sleeping,
And eating strawberries and cream and cakes –
          O cakes, O cakes, O cakes, from Fuller's!
And quite forgetting there's a train to town,
Plotting in an afternoon the new curves for the world.

And peace came. And lying in Sheer
I look round at the corpses of the larches
Whom they slew to make pit-props
For mining the coal for the great armies.
And think, a pit-prop cannot move in the wind,
Nor have red manes hanging in spring from its branches,
And sap making the warm air sweet.
Though you planted it out on the hill again it would be dead.

And if these years have made you into a pit-prop,
To carry the twisting galleries of the world's reconstruction
(Where you may thank God, I suppose
That they set you the sole stay of a nasty corner)
What use is it to you? What use
To have your body lying here
In Sheer, underneath the larches?

JOHN BALABAN

After Our War

After our war, the dismembered bits
— all those pierced eyes, ear slivers, jaw splinters,
gouged lips, odd tibias, skin flaps, and toes —
came squinting, wobbling, jabbering back.
The genitals, of course, were the most bizarre,
inching along roads like glowworms and slugs.
The living wanted them back but good as new.
The dead, of course, had no use for them.
And the ghosts, the tens of thousands of abandoned souls
who had appeared like swamp fog in the city streets,
on the evening altars, and on doorsills of cratered homes,
also had no use for the scraps and bits
because, in their opinion, they looked good without them.
Since all things naturally return to their source,
these snags and tatters arrived, with immigrant uncertainty,
in the United States. It was almost home.
So, now, one can sometimes see a friend or a famous
     man talking
with an extra pair of lips glued and yammering on his cheek,
and this is why handshakes are often unpleasant,
why it is better, sometimes, not to look another in the eye,
why, at your daughter's breast thickens a hard keloidal scar.
After the war, with such Cheshire cats grinning in our trees,
will the ancient tales still tell us new truths?

Will the myriad world surrender new metaphor?
After our war, how will love speak?

1974

Armistice

It is finished. The enormous dust-cloud over Europe
Lifts like a million swallows; and a light
Drifting in craters, touches the quiet dead.

Now, at the bugle's hour, before the blood
Cakes in a clean wind on their marble faces,
Making them monuments; before the sun,

Hung like a medal on the smoky noon,
Whitens the bone that feeds the earth, before
Wheat-ear springs green, again, in the green spring

And they are bread in the bodies of the young:
Be strong to remember how the bread died, screaming;
Gangrene was corn, and monuments went mad.

MICHAEL HAMBURGER

After a War

The outcome? Conflicting rumours
As to what faction murdered
The one who, had he survived,
Might have ruled us without corruption.
Not that it matters now:
We're busy collecting the dead,
Counting them, hard though it is
To be sure what side they were on.
What's left of their bodies and faces
Tells of no need but for burial,
And mutilation was practiced
By Right, Left and Centre alike.
As for the children and women
Who knows what they wanted
Apart from the usual things?
Food is scarce now, and men are scarce,
Whole villages burnt to the ground,
New cities in disrepair.

The war is over. Somebody must have won.
Somebody will have won, when peace is declared.

THOMAS HARDY

'And There Was a Great Calm'

(On the Signing of the Armistice, 11 Nov. 1918)

I

There had been years of Passion – scorching, cold,
And much Despair, and Anger heaving high,
Care whitely watching, Sorrows manifold,
Among the young, among the weak and old,
And the pensive Spirit of Pity whispered, 'Why?'

II

Men had not paused to answer. Foes distraught
Pierced the thinned peoples in a brute-like blindness,
Philosophies that sages long had taught,
And Selflessness, were as an unknown thought,
And 'Hell' and 'Shell!' were yapped at Lovingkindness.

III

The feeble folk at home had grown full-used
To 'dug-outs', 'snipers', 'Huns', from the war-adept
In the mornings heard, and at evetimes perused;
To day-dreamt men in millions, when they mused –
To nightmare-men in millions when they slept.

IV

Waking to wish existence timeless, null,
Sirius they watched above where armies fell;
He seemed to check his flapping when, in the lull
Of night a boom came thencewise, like the dull
Plunge of a stone dropped in some deep well.

V

So, when old hopes that earth was bettering slowly
Were dead and damned, there sounded 'War is done!'
One morrow. Said the bereft, and meek, and lowly,
'Will men some day be given to grace? yea, wholly,
And in good sooth, as our dreams used to run?'

VI

Breathless they paused. Out there men raised their glance
To where had stood those poplars lank and lopped,
As they had raised it through the four years' dance
Of Death in the now familiar flats of France;
And murmured, 'Strange, this! How? All firing stopped?'

VII

Aye; all was hushed. The about-to-fire fired not,
The aimed-at moved away in trance-lipped song,
One checkless regiment slung a clinching shot
And turned. The Spirit of Irony smirked out, 'What?
Spoil peradventures woven of Rage and Wrong?'

VIII

Thenceforth no flying fires inflamed the gray,
No hurtlings shook the dewdrop from the thorn,
No moan perplexed the mute bird on the spray;
Worn horses mused: 'We are not whipped to-day;'
No weft-winged engines blurred the moon's thin horn.

IX

Calm fell. From Heaven distilled a clemency;
There was peace on earth, and silence in the sky;
Some could, some could not, shake off misery:
The Sinister Spirit sneered: 'It had to be!'
And again the Spirit of Pity whispered, 'Why?'

DOUGLAS DUNN

Souvenirs of Versailles

At times like these, fountain pens come into their own.
'Now that your war is lost, and ours is won,
There should be peace in places where there's none.
Orderly! Please, pass me the microphone.'

*

The subalterns clear up. 'They've pinched the pens!
I ask you, Frank. Does that make any sense?'
'Don't fret. I mean, a pen is just a pen.
You never know. They might need them again.'

IVAN V. LALIĆ

The Spaces of Hope

I have experienced the spaces of hope,
The spaces of a moderate mercy. Experienced
The places which suddenly set
Into a random form: a lilac garden,
A street in Florence, a morning room,
A sea smeared with silver before the storm,
Or a starless night lit only
By a book on the table. The spaces of hope
Are in time, not linked into
A system of miracles, nor into a unity;
They merely exist. As in Kanfanar,
At the station; wind in a wild vine
A quarter-century ago: one space of hope.
Another, set somewhere in the future,
Is already destroying the void around it,
Unclear but real. Probable.

In the spaces of hope light grows,
Free of charge, and voices are clearer,
Death has a beautiful shadow, the lilac blooms later,
But for that it looks like its first-ever flower.

translated by FRANCIS R. JONES

ROY McFADDEN

Post-War

Cold and clear are the words
That belong to bright March days,
If you think of mornings
When sky is gunmetal blue
And a terse breeze flexes its strength in the raw trees.

The hard years after the war
When life, in a word, was spare,
Were like March mornings
Cold-shouldered or cut by spring,
Yet with promise, in spite of the promises, sharpening the air.

Remembered merchandise –
Shelved childhood's packets and tins –
Trailed back from limbo,
Nostalgically labelled, and we
Reflected on pots and pans, matched saucers and spoons.

Under the cenotaphs
The poppies foundered on stone;
And over the bomb-holes
Pert window-boxes presumed.
They restored the excursion train and the ice-cream cone.

Then we dallied with summer again,
Making light of the rusting guns,
The snarled wire's venom,
The abandoned towers on the dunes;
And salvaged stray bullets for girls to give to their sons.

CECILY MACKWORTH

En Route

A man in the café laughed and said: the war is done.
The instant froze and joined the starry way
Of clear, unchangeable things men do and say
That spin in whirling history around a tired sun.

Along the roads the tired people lay,
Death's feet were quiet in a sky of indigo,
It seemed an old song of Touraine from long ago
Still lingered in that centuries-old evening, fragile and gay.

The chequered map of France beneath our feet
Unrolled itself day after clover-scented, azure day,
Incarnate Summer's ultimate and proud display
Before she laid her corn and birds and flowers down in defeat.

The Evacuees

There is no sound of guns here, nor echo of guns.
The spasm of bombs has dissolved
Into the determination of the tractor.

Our music now is the rasp of the corncrake
And the wedge-shaped call of the cuckoo
Above leaves tranced in the lap of summer.

We have discovered the grass, curled in the ditches.
We have combed it with rakes in the hayfields,
And coiffed it in lion-coloured stacks.

We have stroked milk, warm and gentle from the cow,
The placid primitive milk, before bottles
Sterilise its mild wonder.

We have met the bland smile of eggs in the willow-basket;
Returned the stolid stare of cheeses ripening on the shelf;
Warmed ourselves at the smell of baking bread.

We have seen food, the sacrament of life,
Not emasculate and defunct upon dishes, but alive,
Springing from the earth after the discipline of the plough.

1945

They came running over the perilous sands
  Children with their golden eyes
Crying: *Look! We have found samphire*
  Holding out their bone-ridden hands.

It might have been the spittle of wrens
  Or the silver nest of a squirrel
For I was invested with the darkness
  Of an ancient quarrel whose omens
Lay scatter'd on the silted beach.
  The children came running toward me

But I saw only the waves behind them
  Cold, salt and disastrous
Lift their black banners and break
  Endlessly, without resurrection.

EDWIN MUIR

The Horses

Barely a twelvemonth after
The seven days war that put the world to sleep,
Late in the evening the strange horses came.
By then we had made our covenant with silence,
But in the first few days it was so still
We listened to our breathing and were afraid.
On the second day
The radios failed; we turned the knobs; no answer.
On the third day a warship passed us, heading north.
Dead bodies piled on the deck. On the sixth day
A plane plunged over us into the sea. Thereafter
Nothing. The radios dumb;
And still they stand in corners of our kitchens,
And stand, perhaps, turned on, in a million rooms
All over the world. But now if they should speak,
If on a sudden they should speak again,
If on the stroke of noon a voice should speak,
We would not listen, we would not let it bring
That old bad world that swallowed its children quick
At one great gulp. We would not have it again.
Sometimes we think of the nations lying asleep,
Curled blindly in impenetrable sorrow,
And then the thought confounds us with its strangeness.

The tractors lie about our fields; at evening
They look like dank sea-monsters couched and waiting.
We leave them where they are and let them rust:
'They'll moulder away and be like other loam'.
We make our oxen drag our rusty ploughs,
Long laid aside. We have gone back
Far past our fathers' land.
                                      And then, that evening
Late in the summer the strange horses came.
We heard a distant tapping on the road,
A deepening drumming; it stopped, went on again
And at the corner changed to hollow thunder.
We saw the heads
Like a wild wave charging and were afraid.
We had sold our horses in our fathers' time
To buy new tractors. Now they were strange to us
As fabulous steeds set on an ancient shield
Or illustrations in a book of knights.
We did not dare go near them. Yet they waited,
Stubborn and shy, as if they had been sent
By an old command to find our whereabouts
And that long-lost archaic companionship.
In the first moment we had never a thought
That they were creatures to be owned and used.
Among them were some half-a-dozen colts
Dropped in some wilderness of the broken world,
Yet new as if they had come from their own Eden.
Since then they have pulled our ploughs and borne our loads,
But that free servitude still can pierce our hearts.
Our life is changed; their coming our beginning.

EDMUND BLUNDEN

Ancre Sunshine

In all his glory the sun was high and glowing
Over the farm world where we found great peace,
And clearest blue the winding river flowing
Seemed to be celebrating a release
From all that speed and music of its own
Which but for some few cows we heard alone.

Here half a century before might I,
Had something chanced, about this point have lain,
Looking with failing sense on such blue sky,
And then became a name with others slain.
But that thought vanished. Claire was wandering free
Miraumont way in the golden tasselled lea.

The railway trains went by, and dreamily
I thought of them as planets in their course,
Thought bound perhaps for Arras, how would we
Have wondered once if through the furious force
Murdering our world one of these same had come,
Friendly and sensible – 'the war's over, chum'.

And now it seemed Claire was afar, and I
Alone, and where she went perhaps the mill
That used to be had rised again, and by
All that had fallen was in its old form still,
For her to witness, with no cold surprise,
In one of those moments when nothing dies.

Armistice

Through steam and woodsmoke
the train slides in.

The boys who stood straight as sugar-cane
have come back changed, spilled

out of carriages, still
wearing the Emperor's uniform.

There are no crowds today,
no brass or beating drums;

only a sullen silence, the sidling
sideways glance, the kind of looks

that shadowed them
in England and through France.

Our letters went back and forth
through the hands of spies,

read by so many eyes the words
were all used up before they arrived.

The enemy who paid their wages
has travelled back with them

and they say the war has ended,
but what kind of peace is this

when the crop is blasted,
home a bitter kiss.

Heroes

This war's dead heroes, who has seen them?
They rise in smoke above the burning city,
Faint clouds, dissolving into sky.

And who sifting the Libyan sand can find
The tracery of a human hand,
The faint impression of an absent mind,
The fade-out of a soldier's day dream?

You'll know your love no more, nor his sweet kisses –
He's forgotten you, girl, and in the idle sun
In long green grass that the east wind caresses
The seed of man is ravished by the corn.

El Alamein

There are flowers now, they say, at Alamein;
Yes, flowers in the minefields now.
So those that come to view that vacant scene,
Where death remains and agony has been
Will find the lilies grow —
Flowers, and nothing that we know.

So they rang the bells for us and Alamein,
Bells which we could not hear:
And to those that heard the bells what could it mean,
That name of loss and pride, El Alamein?
— Not the murk and harm of war,
But their hope, their own warm prayer.

It will become a staid historic name,
That crazy sea of sand!
Like Troy or Agincourt its single fame
Will be the garland for our brow, our claim,
On us a fleck of glory to the end:
And there our dead will keep their holy ground.

But this is not the place that we recall,
The crowded desert crossed with foaming tracks,
The one blotched building, lacking half a wall,
The grey-faced men, sand powdered over all;
The tanks, the guns, the trucks,
The black, dark-smoking wrecks.

So be it: none but us has known that land:
El Alamein will still be only ours
And those ten days of chaos in the sand.
Others will come who cannot understand,
Will halt beside the rusty minefield wires
And find there – flowers.

The Vote

The helmet now an hive for bees becomes,
And hilts of swords may serve for spiders' looms;
    Sharp pikes may make
    Teeth for a rake;
And the keen blade, th'arch enemy of life,
Shall be degraded to a pruning knife.
    The rustic spade
    Which first was made
For honest agriculture, shall retake
Its primitive employment, and forsake
    The rampires steep
    And trenches deep.
Tame conies in our brazen guns shall breed,
Or gentle doves their young ones there shall feed.
    In musket barrels
    Mice shall raise quarrels
For their quarters. The ventriloquious drum,
Like lawyers in vacations, shall be dumb.
    Now all recruits,
    But those of fruits,
Shall be forgot; and th'unarmed soldier
Shall only boast of what he did whilere,
    In chimneys' ends
    Among his friends.

If good effects shall happy signs ensue,
I shall rejoice, and my prediction's true.

Peace Celebration

Now we can say of those who died unsung,
Unwept for, torn, 'Thank God they were not blind
Or mad! They've perished strong and young,
Missing the misery we elders find
In missing them.' With such a platitude
We try to cheer ourselves. And for each life
Laid down for us, with duty well-imbued,
With song-on-lip, in splendid soldier strife –
For sailors, too, who willingly were sunk –
We'll shout 'Hooray!' –
                              And get a little drunk.

DOROTHY UNA RATCLIFFE

Remembrance Day in the Dales

It's a fine kind thought! And yet – I know
The Abbey's not where our Jack should lie,
With his sturdy love of a rolling sky;
   As a tiny child
He loved a sea that was grand and wild.
    God knows best!
Near-by the sea our Jack should rest.

And Willie – Willie our youngest born –
I fear that he might be lonesome, laid
Where the echoing, deep-voiced prayers are said, –
And yet the deep-voiced praying words
Reach God's heart too with the hymns of the birds.
    In His keep
On the edge of a wood our Will should sleep.
    God knows best!
But the years are long since the lads went west.

The Field by the Lirk o' the Hill

Daytime and nicht,
Sun, wind an' rain
The lang cauld licht
O' the spring months again;
The yaird's a' weed
And the fairm's a' still –
Wha'll sow the seed
I' the field by the lirk o' the hill?

Prood maun ye lie,
Prood did ye gang,
Auld, auld am I
And oh! life's lang!
Ghaists i' the air,
Whaups' voices shrill,
And you nae mair
I' the field by the lirk o' the hill –
Aye, bairn, nae mair, nae mair,
I' the field by the lirk o' the hill.

HELEN MORT

Armistice

On the eleventh day
of the eleventh month
I climbed towards Tunnel Mountain.

The snow was the colour
of a clock face, the lodgepole pines
were minute hands – I didn't need the time.

I ignored all paths
and took the closed-off winter road,
walked down the vanished middle, my heart

a ticking engine in my chest
the dipped beam of my stare
but when I heard the silence deepen

on the hour, my body was no machine.
I stopped. The cold was graspable.
I reached out, held it gently by the hand

and stood to face the Rockies
in their regimented lines, the sentry skyline
and the bugle-calls of birds.

I sang *happy birthday*
to your ghost, sang across the continents
to Birmingham, my bad voice

calling out to you, all
that was yours, the war you hardly mentioned,
the buried naval uniform,

the year your pulse failed
and my grandma called a truce,
crossing the miles to speak to you again.

I stood for two minutes,
two hours and when I turned
the snow was falling like dull rain

and though I could not cry
my nose was bleeding
from the sudden height,

the dry and unfamiliar air.
I watched a petal hit the ground
a crimson flower, opening.

KŌICHI IIJIMA

The End of the War to End All Wars

I. A SKY FOR STRANGERS

The birds came down.
They pecked in cracks made in the earth.
Flew hovering
above the unfamiliar roofs.
They seemed uncertain, bewildered.

The sky holds its head
as though it had eaten stone,
plunged now in grief.
The bloodshed's stopped
but all the blood's still circling in the sky
like strangers wondering at the calm.

II. OUT OF THE SAND

Bean-stalks are growing out of the sand,
potatoes too.
He searched.
For the friendly face
that had fallen into the earth.
And then for his own lost face.

Years I lived through
stained with evil
went whipping past my ear.
The calendars shredded, fluttering.

Years when people like wild dogs
in the dug-outs awkwardly
squatted down and wept.

translated by HARRY *and* LYNN GUEST *and* KAJIMA SHŌZŌ

Peace

I

I am as awful as my brother War,
I am the sudden silence after clamour.
I am the face that shows the seamy scar
When blood has lost its frenzy and its glamour.
Men in my pause shall know the cost at last
That is not to be paid in triumphs or tears,
Men will begin to judge the thing that's past
As men will judge it in a hundred years.

Nations! whose ravenous engines must be fed
Endlessly with the father and the son,
My naked light upon your darkness, dread! –
By which ye shall behold what ye have done:
Whereon, more like a vulture than a dove,
Ye set my seal in hatred, not in love.

II

Let no man call me good. I am not blest.
My single virtue is the end of crimes,
I only am the period of unrest,
The ceasing of the horrors of the times;
My good is but the negative of ill,
Such ill as bends the spirit with despair,
Such ill as makes the nations' soul stand still
And freeze to stone beneath its Gorgon glare.

Be blunt, and say that peace is but a state
Wherein the active soul is free to move,
And nations only show as mean or great
According to the spirit then they prove. –
O which of ye whose battle-cry is Hate
Will first in peace dare shout the name of Love?

Admonition to a Chief

Tell him that
We do not wish for greediness
We do not wish that he should curse us
We do not wish that his ears should be hard of hearing
We do not wish that he should call people fools
We do not wish that he should act on his own initiative
We do not wish things done as in Kumasi
We do not wish that it should ever be said
   'I have no time, I have no time'
We do not wish personal abuse
We do not wish personal violence.

GEORGE HERBERT

Peace

Sweet Peace, where dost thou dwell? I humbly crave,
        Let me once know.
    I sought thee in a secret cave,
        And ask'd, if Peace were there.
A hollow wind did seem to answer, No:
        Go seek elsewhere.

I did; and going did a rainbow note:
        Surely, thought I,
    This is the lace of Peace's coat:
        I will search out the matter.
But while I look'd, the clouds immediately
        Did break and scatter.

Then went I to a garden, and did spy
        A gallant flower,
    The Crown imperial: Sure, said I,
        Peace at the root must dwell.
But when I digg'd, I saw a worm devour
        What show'd so well.

At length I met a rev'rend good old man,
Whom when for Peace
I did demand, he thus began:
There was a Prince of old
At Salem dwelt, who liv'd with good increase
Of flock and fold.

He sweetly liv'd; yet sweetness did not save
His life from foes.
But after death out of his grave
There sprang twelve stalks of wheat:
Which many wond'ring at, got some of those
To plant and set.

It prosper'd strangely, and did soon disperse
Through all the earth:
For they that taste it do rehearse,
That virtue lies therein,
A secret virtue bringing peace and mirth
By flight of sin.

Take of this grain, which in my garden grows,
And grows for you;
Make bread of it: and that repose
And peace which ev'ry where
With so much earnestness you do pursue,
Is only there.

A. E. F.

There will be a rusty gun on the wall, sweetheart,
The rifle grooves curling with flakes of rust.
A spider will make a silver string nest in the darkest,
  warmest corner of it.
The trigger and the range-finder, they too will be rusty.
And no hands will polish the gun, and it will hang on
  the wall.
Forefingers and thumbs will point absently and casually
  toward it.
It will be spoken among half-forgotten, wished-to-be-
  forgotten things.
They will tell the spider: Go on, you're doing good work.

MARY STUDD

Paris, 1919

Tune up with the dance of sorrow,
'Tis a measure we all can tread,
Tune up with the dance of sorrow,
We dance on the graves of the dead.

Tune up with the dance of sorrow,
Let the fountain of laughter flow,
We bankrupts may lightly borrow
And carry our loot to the show.

Tune up with the music of sorrow,
Tango and Jazz and song,
We'll be sodden and stiff tomorrow,
But the night of the grave is long.

CONRAD AIKEN

The Quarrel

Suddenly, after the quarrel, while we waited,
Disheartened, silent, with downcast looks, nor stirred
Eyelid nor finger, hopeless both, yet hoping
Against all hope to unsay the sundering word:

While all the room's stillness deepened, deepened about us
And each of us crept his thought's way to discover
How, with as little sound as the fall of a leaf,
The shadow had fallen, and lover quarreled with lover;

And while, in the quiet, I marveled – alas, alas –
At your deep beauty, your tragic beauty, torn
As the pale flower is torn by the wanton sparrow –
This beauty, pitied and loved, and now forsworn;

It was then, when the instant darkened to its darkest, –
When faith was lost with hope, and the rain conspired
To strike its gray arpeggios against our heartstrings, –
When love no longer dared, and scarcely desired:

It was then that suddenly, in the neighbor's room,
The music started: that brave quartette of strings
Breaking out of the stillness, as out of our stillness,
Like the indomitable heart of life that sings

When all is lost; and startled from our sorrow,
Tranced from our grief by that diviner grief,
We raised remembering eyes, each looked at other,
Blinded with tears of joy; and another leaf

Fell silently as that first; and in the instant
The shadow had gone, our quarrel became absurd;
And we rose, to the angelic voices of the music,
And I touched your hand, and we kissed, without a word.

MARY JEAN CHAN

Truce

the Red Guards were snakes / some versions of original sin / the young men had heavy hands / so many fathers falling at the feet of sons / the beloved father my mother lost at the age of eleven / the grandfather I never met / I am my mother's daughter / whose rage is not simple / the women I love / nurse invisible wounds / my love for them is fierce and flares up through the body's / many secret passages / my period is erratic / there must be some form of release / those weeks when my mother / cursed my name in the mirror / unable to stare her own / queer creation in the eye / I had the feeling she was addressing someone else / that the screams / were meant for me / yet somehow misdirected / forgiveness is not simple / our failed attempts at peace / the good enough mothers / I have since sought elsewhere / the letters she writes to me / a Chinese script dashed / so beautifully across the page / I want to kiss our interlocked hands / cherish their painful truce with memory / our ongoing effort at joy / after the long decade of war

The Coming of Good Luck

So good luck came, and on my roof did light,
Like noiseless snow, or as the dew of night:
Not all at once, but gently, as the trees
Are by the sunbeams tickled by degrees.

SEAMUS HEANEY

from The Cure at Troy

Human beings suffer.
They torture one another.
They get hurt and get hard.
No poem or play or song
Can fully right a wrong
Inflicted and endured.

History says, Don't hope
On this side of the grave,
But then, once in a lifetime
The longed-for tidal wave
Of justice can rise up,
And hope and history rhyme.

So hope for a great sea-change
On the far side of revenge.
Believe that a farther shore
Is reachable from here.
Believe in miracles
And cures and healing wells.

Call miracle self-healing,
The utter self-revealing
Double-take of feeling.
If there's fire on the mountain
And lightning and storm
And a god speaks from the sky

That means someone is hearing
The outcry and the birth-cry
Of new life at its term.
It means once in a lifetime
That justice can rise up
And hope and history rhyme.

Prayer

Here I work in the hollow of God's hand
with Time bent round into my reach. I touch
 the circle of the earth, I throw and catch
the sun and moon by turns into my mind.
I sense the length of it from end to end,
I sway me gently in my flesh and each
point of the process changes as I watch;
the flowers come, the rain follows the wind.

And all I ask is this – and you can see
how far the soul, when it goes under flesh,
is not a soul, is small and creaturish –
that every day the sun comes silently
to set my hands to work and that the moon
turns and returns to meet me when it's done.

JO SHAPCOTT

Phrase Book

I'm standing here inside my skin
which will do for a Human Remains Pouch
for the moment. Look down there (up here).
Quickly. Slowly. This is my own front room

where I'm lost in the action, live from a war,
on screen. I am an Englishwoman, I don't understand you.
What's the matter? You are right. You are wrong.
Things are going well (badly). Am I disturbing you?

TV is showing bliss as taught to pilots:
Blend, Low silhouette, Irregular shape, Small,
Secluded. (Please write it down. Please speak slowly.)
Bliss is how it was in this very room

when I raised my body to his mouth,
when he even balanced me in the air,
or at least I thought so and yes the pilots say
yes they have caught it through the Side-Looking

Airborne Radar, and through the J–Stars.
I am expecting a gentleman (a young gentleman,
two gentlemen, some gentlemen). Please send him
(them) up at once. This is really beautiful.

Yes they have seen us, the pilots, in the Kill Box
on their screens, and played the routine for
getting us Stealthed, that is, Cleansed, to you and me,
Taken Out. They know how to move into a single room

like that, to send in with Pinpoint Accuracy, a hundred Harms.
I have two cases and a cardboard box. There is another
bag there. I cannot open my case – look out,
the lock is broken. Have I done enough?

Bliss, the pilots say, is for evasion
and escape. What's love in all this debris?
Just one person pounding another into dust,
into dust. I do not know the word for it yet.

Where is the British Consulate? Please explain.
What does it mean? What must I do? Where
can I find? What have I done? I have done
nothing. Let me pass please. I am an Englishwoman.

Thaw

Over the land freckled with snow half-thawed
The speculating rooks at their nests cawed
And saw from elm-tops, delicate as flower of grass,
What we below could not see, Winter pass.

DEREK WALCOTT

The Season of Phantasmal Peace

Then all the nations of birds lifted together
the huge net of the shadows of this earth
in multitudinous dialects, twittering tongues,
stitching and crossing it. They lifted up
the shadows of long pines down trackless slopes,
the shadows of glass-faced towers down evening streets,
the shadow of a frail plant on a city sill –
the net rising soundless at night, the birds' cries soundless, until
there was no longer dusk, or season, decline, or weather,
only this passage of phantasmal light
that not the narrowest shadow dared to sever.

And men could not see, looking up, what the wild geese drew,
what the ospreys trailed behind them in silvery ropes
that flashed in the icy sunlight; they could not hear
battalions of starlings waging peaceful cries,
bearing the net higher, covering this world
like the vines of an orchard, or a mother drawing
the trembling gauze over the trembling eyes
of a child fluttering to sleep;
                                        it was the light
that you will see at evening on the side of a hill
in yellow October, and no one hearing knew
what change had brought into the raven's cawing,
the killdeer's screech, the ember-circling chough

such an immense, soundless, and high concern
for the fields and cities where the birds belong,
except it was their seasonal passing, Love,
made seasonless, or, from the high privilege of their birth,
something brighter than pity for the wingless ones
below them who shared dark holes in windows and in houses,
and higher they lifted the net with soundless voices
above all change, betrayals of falling suns,
and this season lasted one moment, like the pause
between dusk and darkness, between fury and peace,
but, for such as our earth is now, it lasted long.

PAUL MULDOON

Armistice Day

In a northern forest the very ravens
were flagging as you raised another glass
of the *rakija* you'd inherited from that dodgy Sarajevan.
Until last night the only song you'd sung
was granite, granite, granite.
Even then we were far from close
to finding common ground.
You looked beyond this unlikely haven
to wonder how the negotiators could be clean-shaven.
Perhaps a distant captain would give tongue
to a hope to which you'd clung.

This morning there's a gearing
up to settle on a single term
for 'a forest clearing
that will accommodate a high-strung
railway car'.
That car is lodged here as Saint Fiacre's arm
is lodged within its arm-shaped reliquary.
We look beyond the goal to which we're steering
to wonder if it isn't met by veering.
Perhaps a distant patois will give tongue
to a hope to which we've clung.

Far to the south, among the wolf-infested
dunes and salt-ponds
of Landes, two sheepskin-vested
shepherds will climb down from their single-rung
five-foot pine stilts
long enough to suspend
hostilities.
They'll look beyond the scrub they've readily breasted
to wonder if they've finally been bested.
Perhaps a distant she-wolf will give tongue
to a hope to which they've clung.

where's.

a nation building itself to rubble's on the screen,
in the Slug & Lettuce where I sup ale
and await my lover. Subtitles for the news
glow, are on the hoof, come up like odd
bricks
for the voice-over that reveals a lull, perhaps
ceasefire. The camera runs for a hole down a mountain
past sandbags: a hospital!
The low ceiling seems imploded with grey clouds –
the bobbly arenas
of the cave. The 'beds' in row have today's threadbare –
it's a boy, a green bruise, no, an
eye is rolled into weird zoom, it seems to say: *where's my gran*
-ddad, where's. Let's assume it's his last
lint-line to himself years after the intrigue
deepened, a thought which carries us, slow
pan-shot, toward his good arm, it's stretched outwards
          like the loose cable above him.
Does that cable hover, snake-like,
from a previous situation? Fanatic cave!
In the frame, both viper and arm
are reaching forwards for the word
where which is left behind on this sports screen.
Oh someone, please help them
roly-poly back to an age of granddads and gardens!

EMILY DICKINSON

'Hope' is the thing with feathers

'Hope' is the thing with feathers –
That perches in the soul –
And sings the tune without the words –
And never stops – at all –

And sweetest – in the Gale – is heard –
And sore must be the storm –
That could abash the little Bird
That kept so many warm –

I've heard it in the chillest land –
And on the strangest Sea –
Yet, never, in Extremity,
It asked a crumb – of Me.

A Churchyard Song of Patient Hope

All tears done away with the bitter unquiet sea,
    Death done away from among the living at last,
Man shall say of sorrow – Love grant it to thee and me! –
        At last, 'It is past.'

Shall I say of pain, 'It is past,' nor say it with thee,
    Thou heart of my heart, thou soul of my soul, my Friend?
Shalt thou say of pain, 'It is past,' nor say it with me
        Beloved to the end?

One woe is past. Come what come will
    Thus much is ended and made fast:
Two woes may overhang us still;
    One woe is past.

    As flowers when winter puffs its last
Wake in the vale, trail up the hill,
    Nor wait for skies to overcast;

So meek souls rally from the chill
    Of pain and fear and poisonous blast,
To lift their heads: come good, come ill,
    One woe is past.

EDWARD THOMAS

Adlestrop

Yes. I remember Adlestrop –
The name, because one afternoon
Of heat the express-train drew up there
Unwontedly. It was late June.

The steam hissed. Someone cleared his throat.
No one left and no one came
On the bare platform. What I saw
Was Adlestrop – only the name

And willows, willow-herb, and grass,
And meadowsweet, and haycocks dry,
No whit less still and lonely fair
Than the high cloudlets in the sky.

And for that minute a blackbird sang
Close by, and round him, mistier
 Farther and farther, all the birds
Of Oxfordshire and Gloucestershire.

Quiver

An Irishman in the British Army
in exchange for three meals a day.
Or, an Irish boy maybe, five foot five,
lying about his age, hungry. An Irish boy.
Ypres, Somme, Abancourt.

An Irishman in the British Army
'of good character', disciplined for drink
when his father dies in the workhouse,
'of good character', confined to barracks
when Casement is hanged.

An Irishman in the British Army, released.
A girl in the steam of a soup kitchen
– the room quivers – a girl through steam
lifts her head to look back at him.
Swimmily. She'll do fine. It's time.

He pictures her, steady at a stove somewhere,
they'll plant a row of scallions, lilies maybe,
watch the waves from a shore he can't name,
through steam he pictures her steady,
somewhere. A quiver. It's time.

An Irishman in the British Army
never to be welcomed home, sees Ireland
just once more, swimmily, would not picture
me, a little way down the line somewhere,
looking back at him, released.

W. B. YEATS

The Lake Isle of Innisfree

I will arise and go now, and go to Innisfree,
And a small cabin build there, of clay and wattles made:
Nine bean-rows will I have there, a hive for the honey-bee,
And live alone in the bee-loud glade.

And I shall have some peace there, for peace comes dropping slow,
Dropping from the veils of the morning to where the cricket sings;
There midnight's all a glimmer, and noon a purple glow,
And evening full of the linnet's wings.

I will arise and go now, for always night and day
I hear lake water lapping with low sounds by the shore;
While I stand on the roadway, or on the pavements grey,
I hear it in the deep heart's core.

The Return

We have been off on a long voyage, have we not?
Have done and seen much in that time, but have got

Little that you will prize, who are dancing now
In the silent town whose lights gleam back from our prow.

For you we have brought no pearls or gold, you will learn,
And the best we have brought for ourselves is our glad return.

We bless the estuary lying quiet in the dark,
We praise the power that is given us to steer our barque,

With the old delight, with the sense of a brief reprieve,
Up by the snowy docks on Christmas Eve.

And though you have turned for us, and have taken your release
From us and all thought of us, yet on this night of peace

Pause for a moment, put by your dance and song:
Take to us kindly, and we shall not stay long.

We shall dock the ship, and loose the dogs to roam
And across the fallen snow shall come to our home.

The music will pause, and you will hear our knock
On the door of our home. Open. We shall not mock

Anything you may do in this sacred place.
But look for a moment, and try to recall our face,

Remember on Christmas Eve, as you stand in the doorway there
And regard us as strangers, the forgotten love we bear,

And shall bear it always over the frozen snow
When the door is shut again, and once again we go.

The souls of the forgotten, for whom there is no repose
When the music begins again, and again the doors close,

For whom a thought of yours would come the length
Of a whole dark hemisphere to give us strength.

The souls of the forgotten: others reign in our stead,
But let us go with at least your blessing on our head,

Who year after year shall creep, forgotten lover and bride,
To your door and knock, and knock, at every Christmastide,

Who, lost and ever-rejected, turn from your door and weep,
And retrace our steps to the harbour, where it lies silent and deep

In a slumber of snow and starlight. This is the scene we know
And shall bear in our hearts for ever as worlds away we go:

The harbour, the town, the dancing: to which the soul returns,
Lost and ever-rejected, under a Star which burns

In the zenith over the mainmast. And again it is Christmas morn,
And again in the snow and the Star's light, once again we are born.

1944

ROBERT BURNS

Auld Lang Syne

Should auld acquaintance be forgot
   And never brought to mind?
Should auld acquaintance be forgot,
   And auld lang syne!

For auld lang syne, my jo,
   For auld lang syne,
We'll tak a cup o' kindness yet
   For auld lang syne.

And surely ye'll be your pint stowp!
   And surely I'll be mine!
And we'll tak a cup o' kindness yet,
   For auld lang syne.

    For auld lang syne, my jo, . . .

We twa hae run about the braes
   And pou'd the gowans fine;
But we've wander'd many a weary fitt,
   Sin auld lang syne.

    For auld lang syne, my jo, . . .

We twa hae paidl'd in the burn
    Frae morning sun till dine;
But seas between us braid hae roar'd,
    Sin auld lang syne.

       For auld lang syne, my jo, . . .

And there's a hand, my trusty fiere!
    And gie's a hand o' thine!
And we'll tak a right gude-willie-waught,
    For auld lang syne

       For auld lang syne, my jo, . . .

SEIICHI NIIKUNI

Anti-War

反 = anti   戦 = war   又 = again

Poppy

Who crops up wherever ground is opened, broken . . .
No, this is not enough.

Who crops up where acidic ground is neutralised – in Belgium
blasted bones and rubble added their twist of lime
turning the disturbed earth red . . .
No, this is not enough.

Then where seeds lay buried, dormant – those older than I am,
catching light, can stir from their long sleep in time,
like history, raising a hand, a head . . .
No, this is not enough.

Remember? Who's there in the first script, on a Mesopotamian
tablet: *Hul* and *Gil* – 'joy flower' – a cuneiform
cocktail, our earliest remedy . . .

Who begot war in China, was named by Arabs *Abou-el-noum*,
'father of sleep'; a bloody sign of love's martyrdom –
gul-e-lala – 'flower of red', in Persian and Urdu . . .

Remember? Beloved of Persephone; also found in the tomb –
like a watch, worn on the wrist – of Tutankhamun,
and on coins issued by Herod . . .
No, this is not enough.

You need more? . . . Who crops up, fringing the banks of Lethe
after Troy; who bridges forgetfulness and memory,
life and death, relief and pain . . .

Who was loved by Coleridge who wished *I could wrap up the view*
from my House in a pill of opium & send it to you – to be
seen, swallowed, whole again . . .
No, this is not enough.

Who is the *minded flower* Shakespeare partly saw, in all
        the drowsy
syrups of the world – a release from grief that calls for more
far-fetched relief, and, as morphine,

sent your sap through my mother's veins, while she could
        hear me,
while warmth remained in those hands that first held me,
first calmed my small, fevered brain . . .
No, this is not enough.

Whose pupil is a void dilating with light, its first and last entry –
a compound eye, in whichever form – who sees
the black dot of the beginning . . .

Who's there on that date when all the 1s meet, looped in a wreath
year upon year, or poked through the eye
of a buttonhole. There. I'm done . . .
No, this is not enough.

Then: *Mother — Mother —* last word of that bleeding,
    wrecked soldier,
as heard by the last Tommy, the last link to living memory —
spoken for now, like the countless millions

of mouthless dead. There in the underworld. The fallen, heavy
head. The deaths we live with. Enough said. Remember?
This is you. Wake up. You're summoned.

No, this is not enough.

Outlook Tower

Stars in the night sky, ants in the earth
Birds on their winter way
Trees in the forest
Babies in a womb
Cells in a bloodstream
X or Y in the chromosome, in the alphabet,
Rivers running into the sea
You Sassoon, you, Wilfred Owen
You flute, you cymbal, you bassoon,
You Pluto, you Mars, you moon,
You love, my dear, my darling,
You world, you precious earth
You beloved field, you forever Scotland,
You foreign face, you looking glass,
You microcosm, you black hole, you star,
You lad, you lass, you water, you fire.
You you you you you, just as you are.

ACKNOWLEDGEMENTS

The editor and publishers gratefully acknowledge permission to reprint copyright material in this book, as follows:

SIEGFRIED SASSOON: 'Everyone Sang', copyright © Siegfried Sassoon. Reprinted by kind permission of the Estate of George Sassoon, c/o Barbara Levy Literary Agency

RUTH PITTER: 'The Military Harpist', from *The Spirit Watches*, The Cresset Press, 1939. Reprinted by permission of the Estate of the author

MAHMOUD DARWISH: 'Murdered and Unknown', translated by Fady Joudah. Reprinted by permission of the Estate of the author and the translator Dr Fady Joudah

WISŁAWA SZYMBORSKA: 'The End and the Beginning' from *Poems: New and Collected 1957–1997*, Faber & Faber Ltd, 1998; and *View with a Grain of Sand: Selected Poems*, translated from Polish by Stanisław Barańczak and Clare Cavanagh, 1995. Copyright © 1976 by Czytelnik. Reprinted by permission of the publisher and Houghton Mifflin Harcourt Publishing Company. All rights reserved

IVOR GURNEY: 'The Bugle'. Reprinted by permission of The Ivor Gurney Trust

MAY WEDDERBURN CANNAN: 'For a Girl' from *The Splendid Days: Poems*, Blackwell, 1919. Reprinted with kind permission from the Estate of the author

IOAN ALEXANDRU: 'The End of the War' translated by Andrea Deletant and Brenda Walker from *An Anthology of Contemporary Romanian Poetry*, 1996, Forest Books London. Reprinted with kind permission of Andrea Deletant and Brenda Walker

SARAH MAGUIRE: 'The Pomegranates of Kandahar' from *The Pomegranates of Kandahar*, Chatto, copyright © 2007. Reprinted by permission of The Random House Group Limited

CAROLA OMAN: 'Ambulance Train 30', Oman Productions. Reprinted with kind permission of Roy Strong

ALAN GILLIS: 'Progress' from *Somebody, Somewhere*, 2004. Reprinted by the kind permission of the author and The Gallery Press, Loughcrew, Oldcastle, County Meath, Ireland

JOHN HEWITT: from *Freehold*, 1944. Reprinted by permission of the Trustees of the author's Estate

JOHN BALABAN: 'In Celebration of Spring' from *Locusts at the Edge of Summer, New and Selected Poems*, Copper Canyon, 2003, © 1997. Reprinted by permission of The Permissions Company on behalf of the author

CHARLES CAUSLEY: 'At the British War Cemetery, Bayeux' from *Collected Poems 1951–2000*, Macmillan. Reprinted by permission of David Higham Associates Ltd

SEAN O'BRIEN: 'The Sunken Road', copyright © 2018 by Sean O'Brien

SIEGFRIED SASSOON: 'Reconciliation', copyright © Siegfried Sassoon. Reprinted by kind permission of the Estate of George Sassoon, c/o Barbara Levy Literary Agency

ROBERT GRAVES: 'Two Fusiliers' from *The Completed Poems in One Volume*. Reprinted by permission of Carcanet Press Limited

PAUL MULDOON: 'Truce' from *New Selected Poems 1968–1994*, Faber & Faber Ltd, 2004. Reprinted by permission of the publisher

SIMON ARMITAGE: 'The Handshake', copyright © 2018 by Simon Armitage

DANIELA GIOSEFFI: 'To an Army Wife in Sardis' from *Women on War: An International Anthology of Writings from Antiquity to the Present*, 2nd edition by Daniela Gioseffi, copyright © 2003. Reprinted by permission of Daniela Gioseffi

SAADI YOUSSEF: 'Night in Al-Hamra', translated by Khaled Mattawa from *Without an Alphabet, Without a Face*, Graywolf Press, 2003. Reprinted by permission of The Permissions Company on behalf of the author and Khaled Mattawa

INDEX OF AUTHORS

INDEX OF TITLES AND FIRST LINES

163

When you are standing at your hero's grave 40
where's. 135
Who crops up wherever ground is opened, broken 148
Who was it who suggested that the opposite of war 73
Word over all, beautiful as the sky 41

Yes. I remember Adlestrop 138